Chronicles Of Quiet Souls

Ipsita Datta

Dedication

To the dreamers and wanderers

Preface

In a world brimming with noise and ceaseless movement, poetry has always offered me a sanctuary—a quiet space to reflect, question, and reimagine. This collection of twenty-one poems emerged from moments both fleeting and profound, each an exploration of the threads that bind our inner and outer worlds.

These poems are not merely words on a page but conversations with time, memory, and the elements that shape us. They speak of longing and discovery, silence and resonance, weaving together fragments of the everyday with whispers of the universal.

My hope is that these verses invite you into their folds, sparking reflections of your own journeys and emotions. May you find in these words a mirror, a window, or perhaps just a moment of stillness in the chaos.

Acknowledgements

This book would not have come into being without the unwavering support of those who have journeyed alongside me.

To my family, who nurtured my earliest love of language and creativity, thank you for your encouragement and belief in me. To my friends, who have always been there to listen, share, and inspire, your presence has been a constant source of joy and strength.

To those unnamed but not forgotten—strangers, fleeting encounters, and moments of serendipity that inspired these verses—thank you for coloring my world.

Lastly, to the readers who hold this book in their hands, you are the reason these words take flight. Thank you for walking this path with me.

I. The Moon and Her Stars

The moon ascends, a solitary light,
Quietly ruling the velvet night.
She glows not with the sun's fierce fire,
Yet holds a charm, serene, entire.

The stars around, they whisper low,
In clusters bright, their warmth they show.
But still, the moon, steadfast and high,
Shines her path across the sky.

She hears their songs, their gentle call,
Yet feels no envy, none at all.
For though she moves in her own space,
Her glow reflects a timeless grace.

The stars may laugh, the stars may dance,
In shared orbits, a cosmic romance.
But the moon knows what they can't see—
Her solitude holds eternity.

When clouds obscure and nights are long,
Her quiet strength hums its own song.
A beacon, still, for those who stray,
Guiding hearts that lose their way.

For the moon, though lone, is never lost,
Her light undimmed by time or frost.
In her orbit, she finds her part—
A universe within her heart.

II. Wanderer's Soliloquy

A girl with wander in her soul,
She traveled lands, she made them whole,
Collected stories, hearts, and songs,
Danced with strangers, rights and wrongs.

In bustling streets and whispered nights,
She felt the world in colored lights,
Learning ways she couldn't know,
In foreign hands, her spirit'd glow.

But in an alien town she stood,
Lost in corners, misunderstood,
Her memories drifted, cold and stark,
In silent rooms that held no spark.

She'd known the warmth of every face,
Yet found no arms in this strange place,
And wondered if the path she chose
Had left her locked, the doors all closed.

"Did I not live, and laugh, and love,
Or trace my dreams to stars above?"
She sighed, and whispered, bold and free,
"Do what makes you happy—be."

III. I am Enough

I am enough to take a walk
through a crowd that stares at me.
I am enough to sit in fine dining
and ask for a portion of one.

I am happy to enjoy the hustle and bustle
around me while sipping a single glass of wine.
I am enough to walk the beautiful lanes,
to bask in the glory of sunlight,
to smell the fresh dew drops.
I am enough to be the fun lone dancer.

But do not mistake this
for me accepting myself as forlorn.
I am enough for this blissful solitude.

Yet someday, when I start forgetting,
I hope you remind me:
I was enough
before you came along.

IV. What do you want to fight for?

What do you want to fight for?
Women's rights?
Gender rights?
Sexual rights?

What do you want to fight for?
Labour laws?
Education?
Environment?

What do you want to fight for?
Love?
Boundaries?
Values?

What do you want to fight for?
House?
Clothes?
Food?
Bed?

What do you want to fight for?
Community?
Family?
Individual?

One day, when all these battles
are won,
we will discover
another reason to fight.

V. Storm Rider

An awakened day awaits your glory.
An awakened day awaits your fury.

You took us by storm,
you took us by love.
Who art thou
in such a pretty cove?

Open your arms
to the light of the sun,
'Cause today,
you have to let the candlelight burn.

Take away the darkness,
'Cause we want to believe again—
You are there,
you are here.

Take away the grief.
I know the feeling
when your breath smears.

The shadow looms
in the darkness of the night,
But you guide us through
the profane sight.

VI. Dear Best Friend

It's 2:00 a.m., and still, the lights aren't out.
I just keep thinking—
Is it happening?
Is she going away?

I'm gonna miss the talks,
I'm gonna miss the walks,
But mostly,
I'm gonna miss our drunk night-outs.

I'm gonna miss the trips we took,
Gonna miss the crazy looks,
But mostly,
I'll miss the late-night poops.

I search for our pics together—
Alas, there aren't enough.
We preferred to make memories,
And damn, they were tough.

I'll miss your strong words
When I took the fall.
God, please help her
When she hits a similar wall.

You were my agony aunt
And my fortune-teller.
It's time to saddle up, my friend;
You're going to a world full of answers.

This is an ode to my dear tall friend,
I hope our small chats never end.
I'll miss you and love you
Till I see you again.

I sent this to her, and tears fell down.
I faked a smile and wished her
A prosperous now.

VII. Becoming

At three, she twirled with the wind,
bare feet kissed by the earth,
her laughter an anthem of freedom.
At thirty, she walks straight lines,
heels striking echoes of purpose—
or is it the weight of expectation?

They told her her worth:
the keeper, the nurturer, the bride.
She shattered the mold,
but in the shards, she wonders:

What is it to be a woman?
Is it joy, untamed and fleeting?
Or is it nothing
until hands cradle a child,
until vows bind her to a name?

She stands in the duality—
a goddess of creation,
a warrior of choice.

Her beauty aches,
her strength burns,
and in the quiet,
she desires to be whole.

VIII. Small Worlds

We were once endless summers,
barefoot races on sunlit streets,
dreams spilling out like marbles,
rolling too far to catch.

Now, we are adults—
islands adrift in oceans of time,
living in small worlds of solitude,
walls painted with the hues of quiet.

I sip my tea,
and the scent pulls a memory—
laughter tangled in dusk,
voices rising like fireflies,
flickering,
fading.

Nostalgia seeps in,
a gentle ache for what was
and what can never return.
The streets we ran are silent now,
echoes lost to the years.

We built castles in the air,
but time turned them to mist.
And though we live apart,
I wonder—
Do you feel it too?

The yearning for a moment
when we were infinite,
when the world was ours,
and solitude was just
a word we didn't yet know.

IX. Rooted in Myself

Did I ever fall in love with myself?
This body,
a landscape shaped by storms,
its valleys soft, its peaks unyielding,
its rivers of strength flowing quietly beneath.

The rebel in me,
a wildfire that fought to survive,
never knowing she was the earth too—
not just a force,
but a being to be nurtured,
to be loved.

I've spent too long waiting—
for the sun of another's approval
to warm my soil.
But don't I know?
This ground, cracked and aching,
still blooms when I let it.

Did I ever fall in love with myself?
Perhaps not yet.

X. The Wistful One

Amid a sea of shallow laughter,
where words skim the surface
and touch nothing below,
a soul drifts quietly,
searching for depth
in the echo of hollow tides.

The faces around gleam bright,
reflections of fleeting truths,
sparkling for a moment
only to vanish like foam
on the crest of an indifferent wave.

Beneath the noise lies a wish—
for a current that runs deep,
a hand that steadies,
a voice that speaks
not to impress, but to connect.

The soul wonders—
is there one among the many
who sees the stillness,
feels the weight of unspoken words,
and holds them gently,
without fear of their shadows?

Though surrounded by mirages,
the search remains—
for a bond untarnished by pretense,
for a kindred soul
to anchor the wanderer's heart
in a sea of shifting sands.

XI. To My Not-So-Young Brother

You, my not-so-young brother,
have grown in quiet ways—
not with words,
but with the weight of the unspoken,
a presence steady and strong,
built on expectations.

Our bond is a dance of silence,
jabs that bruise but never break,
support that speaks louder
than any words we've learned to share.

I see you,
even when I don't say it.
The boy who used to chase shadows
now casts his own—
strong, steady,
but sometimes too heavy
for one so young at heart.

You wear responsibility
like an armor,
polished and impenetrable.

Does it weigh on you,
this role thrust upon your shoulders,
a mantle of strength
that leaves no room for cracks?

If I have ever been the voice of command,
know it came from love,
from a sister who forgets
that the boy has grown
and must now find his own path.

I want you to know—
it's okay to let go sometimes,
to stumble, to fall.
Even pillars need rest,
and the world will still stand
because your heart built it,
not just your hands.

So, here's to you,
my not-so-young brother,
who fights battles I may never know,
but whose strength and growth
I see in every quiet moment.

XII. The Privilege of Thought

In a world of ticking clocks,
there are those who plant their feet
on solid ground,
while others run on spinning wheels—
moving, moving,
but never arriving.

Some sit beneath trees,
pondering the wind's direction,
while others chop wood to feed the fire,
their sweat the only story
they have time to tell.

What a privilege it is,
to question, to wonder—
to let the mind stretch like a bird
against the horizon,
to wander not out of necessity
but for the sheer joy of it.

Yet beneath this soaring sky,
the earth groans under weight.
Not everyone has the luxury of flight.

Some dig their hands into the soil,
chained by the need to survive,
their dreams buried
beneath the next meal.

The rat race spins faster,
capitalism's great machinery
turning souls into cogs,
worth measured in numbers,
identity stamped with a barcode.
Get rich, get woke,
get noticed,
they whisper—
a hymn for those
with time to listen.

But what of the ones
who wake to labor,
who dream only of rest?
Will they ever taste the quiet joy
of being still,
of letting the mind
be more than a tool?
In this great dance of progress,
some are choreographers,
others the floor they tread upon.

What is a thought,
a question,
a dream,
if not a privilege born
of borrowed time?

The stars shine for everyone,
but not all can look up.

XIII. Eternal Yet Ignored

The sun rises, painting the sky—
a quiet masterpiece, unnoticed.
Dusk whispers in amber and violet,
its colors fading into forgetfulness.

The moon casts its reflection
on a still lake,
a silver secret shared
with no one listening.

Trees sway, rivers hum,
stars blink in ancient rhythms.
Nature offers its beauty each day,
soft and unannounced,
a gift we fail to unwrap.

We, the hurried,
the distracted,
take for granted
what asks for nothing—
yet gives everything.

XIV. The Ones Before Us

They were like us once—
ambitious, wild with dreams,
their hearts ignited
by the flare of possibilities.
They stood where we stand now,
peering into the unknown,
their futures unwritten,
their paths unpaved.

Then came the weight—
small hands to hold,
smaller voices to soothe.
They traded dreams for duty,
restless nights for quiet sacrifices,
always hoping we wouldn't notice
the cost of their love.

Did we ever stop to wonder?
What it meant for them
to carry us through their storms,
to figure it out
without a guide,
to stumble,
to fall,

but always rise
so we could walk steady?

Generations shift like seasons.
They watched their world change,
struggling to bridge the gap
between what they knew
and what we demanded.
Still, they gave all they could—
not always perfectly,
but always with their whole hearts.

Their dreams became our freedom.
Their sacrifices built our wings.
And as we soar,
do we remember
the ones who stayed grounded
to keep us aloft?

XV. The Pull of Opposites

In the city, life hums—
a restless symphony of footsteps,
horns, and hurried hearts.
We chase dreams on concrete paths,
fueled by the energy
that never sleeps.

Yet, the mountains call—
their quiet whispers a balm
for weary souls.
The air is lighter,
the pace slower,
and for a moment,
we remember what stillness feels like.

In the small towns,
life moves gently,
a river unhurried by time.
Familiar faces,
silent streets,
a comfort woven into every corner.
But the city pulls,
its energy electric,
a reminder of what we could become.

And so, we journey—
not always knowing
if it's the stillness we seek,
or the motion,
if it's the solace of the mountain
or the buzz of the streets
that will finally fill us.

Perhaps it's neither.
Perhaps it's the journey itself—
the moments between worlds,
the spaces where we wonder,
the rhythm we find
only in the act of traversing.

To live is to travel,
between chaos and calm,
between longing and belonging,
forever searching,
forever moving.

XVI. Roots and Wings

Caught between two worlds,
one where roots lie,
deep and familiar,
where the earth whispers names
but no longer holds them tight,
and another,
where new roots try to take hold,
the soil foreign,
its embrace tentative.

A tree uprooted,
carrying fragments of one home
while reaching for another.
The winds of longing pull both ways,
and the question lingers—
is there a place
where rest feels true?

They say to belong to oneself,
but what of the days
when silence becomes a burden,
when the weight of being enough
feels insurmountable?

What of the nights
when stars reflect back
only the vastness of wandering?

Belonging becomes a balancing act—
the ache of roots left behind,
the hope of wings not yet sure.
And perhaps,
for those who journey,
home is neither here nor there,
but somewhere in between.

XVII. The Fading Forest

Once, this forest thrived—
roots deep, canopies wide,
branches reaching toward endless skies.
Its whispers danced with the wind,
its presence unshakable,
a world unto itself.

But now, the trees grow weary,
their trunks creak under the weight of years.
The shadows grow longer,
the soil thinner,
and the whispers fade.

The forest wonders—
what happens when no one remembers?
When the birds have flown,
the trails are overgrown,
and its once-vivid greens
are swallowed by silence?

It still shelters a circle of saplings,
young and vibrant,
but their shade can only reach so far.
Can they hold the roots steady

when the storms come?
Can they care for the elder oaks,
or will the winds
pull everything apart?

The forest fears its own fading—
to become a memory,
a place unseen,
a story untold.
Should it give its final strength
to guarding the soil,
or let its roots reach out
to chase the sunlight one last time?

Tired, it stands still,
unsure of the path.
Should it grow for the sky,
or dig deeper into the earth?
Is it enough to exist,
knowing the day will come
when even the tallest tree falls?

The forest dreams of safety,
but longs for freedom.
Can its roots hold steady,
while its branches reach for the sky,
before it fades into the horizon?

XVIII. The Quiet Ascent

With every truth uncovered,
a step further from the crowd—
what once felt close
now drifts like a fading shore.

Ideas build mountains,
but few climb beside you.
The summit offers clarity,
yet leaves you longing
for the warmth of simpler heights.

Each step upward feels lighter,
but the air grows thinner,
the voices below softer,
until the silence greets you,
a companion you never sought.

XIX. The Lost Compass

Belonging, once a steady anchor,
now drifts like a ship unmoored.
The past calls softly,
its voice woven with the scent of old rain,
the echoes of familiar laughter.

The new feels distant,
a land not yet lived in,
its soil foreign,
its language still strange.
Why does one cling to the old,
while trying to shape a life anew?

Nostalgia seeps in—
a shadow of warmth,
a tether to what once was whole.
It whispers of a time
when belonging wasn't a question,
but a quiet truth.

Will it ever return?
Will the pieces of two worlds
fuse into one?
Or will the heart forever wander,
pulled between then and now,
forever searching
for the place it calls home?

XX. Milestones

The road stretches,
paved with expectations,
each mile marked by a stone,
etched with what we must achieve
by when,
and how.

Do they see it?
How these markers,
meant to guide,
become chains
for those who stray too far,
too fast,
too slow.

The highway is straight,
unforgiving,
its milestones immovable,
as if progress could be measured
only in the distance between stones.

But what of the paths
that veer off into the wild?
Where no markers tell you

where you stand,
or if you're enough?
Is the journey less worthy
when it has no map?

I wonder,
who decides what counts?
Who carves the stone
and names it progress?
Does the river question its flow,
or the stars their scattered dance?

Yet, as the sun dips low,
casting shadows long and soft,
a thought takes root—
Perhaps the milestones aren't prisons,
but whispers,
asking only to be reimagined.

Maybe the roads we make,
wild and winding,
are milestones enough—
each step,
each pause,
a story written
in our own language.

And at the end of the highway,
when the stones disappear,
what remains
is the journey
that was ours alone.

XXI. Twilight's Embrace

The day folds itself into twilight's arms,
its edges softened by the hush of stars.
The moon rises,
a quiet sentinel of dreams,
its light a balm
for the weariness we carry.

I close my eyes
and let the world dissolve,
its noise fading
into the rhythm of my breath.
In this stillness,
I find pieces of myself,
scattered by the day,
gathered by the night.

The rebel rests,
the seeker pauses,
the heart,
so often heavy,
finds a moment to float.

Goodnight,
to the battles fought,
to the unspoken fears,
to the dreams deferred
but not forgotten.

Goodnight,
to the stars above,
to the quiet within,
to a self
learning to begin again.